One Wave at a Time

A Story About Grief and Healing

Holly Thompson

ILLUSTRATED BY
Ashley Crowley

Albert Whitman & Company
Chicago, Illinois

we used to be four
Mom, Dad
Ben and me

now we are three
Mom
Ben and me

sadness
comes and goes
in waves

there are places
where Dad
used to be

at the table for dinner
on the sofa napping
on the stoop with his guitar

in the car next to Mom
on the sidelines at games
or waiting with Ben

when sad waves roll in
too many, too fast
I dive under my bed

with a flashlight
a pile of comics
and Dad's green shirt

down there it's a submarine
quiet and safe
beneath stormy waves

along with sad waves
come mad waves
towering and strong

cresting
like tsunamis
and crashing ashore—

Ben throws his toys
Mom yells at the ceiling
I wreck Dad's guitar

some waves
are fear waves
that curl me in a ball

will Mom…? did Dad…?
could I have…?
should I not have…?

fear waves leave
fear stones that make
my stomach ache

some days
there are no waves
just flatness

I'm like a robot
as I ride the bus, walk the halls
sit at my desk

voices seem far
my body is slow
the world is away

happy waves too
slip in to tickle
and tackle

when Mom smiles
or my team scores a goal
or when I play boats with Ben

some happy waves
stay awhile—
others rush away

waves of all kinds
tumble in
one after another

in no special order
unpredictable
as the sea

waves barely there
waves I can ride
waves that break and crash

but lately we join
other families
tumbled by waves

MEMORIES

SAD

PAIN

ANGER

STRENGTH

in groups, we talk and play
and when the question ball asks
what do you miss?

I say *my dad's songs*
and the way he sang them
slow and full of blues

we talk about death—
what it is
and how it happens

our talking stick traveling
the circle as we share
how our special person died

strangers become friends
friends help strangers—
in groups, we ride the waves

at home, we make some changes—
move furniture, hang memory flags
fix Dad's guitar

I fill a grief first aid kit
with things that soothe—
putty, soft cloth, smooth stones

and we add to memory boxes—
Dad's guitar picks
shells, funny jokes he told

sometimes we talk about Dad—
say things we never said
ask things we never asked

or we hold hands
sing *Lean on Me*—
even Ben joining in

or we're quiet
just breathing together—
Mom, Ben, and me

one day we rescue
a chair from the trash
clean it up, paint it fresh

so now on special days
when people visit
we eat Dad foods, sing Dad songs

tell Dad stories
and share Dad memories
in the Memory Chair

when Mom cries now, I don't hide
when Ben whines now, I don't (usually) yell
and when I spy a wave, I inhale slow

the waves still come—
sad waves, mad waves
flat waves and fear waves

but when they roll in
I surf them
one wave at a time

Author's Note

You may have experienced the death of someone close to you. Or a friend or relative may have experienced a death.

When someone close to us dies, we grieve. Grief is "all of the thoughts, feelings, and reactions we have when a special person dies."[1] Grief may include many different feelings—sadness, anger, guilt, hurt, fear, regret, worry, relief, numbness, shame, and exhaustion. These feelings may be all mixed up, and they may hit us in waves. Grief feelings and reactions may come to us soon after a person dies, or they may come to us much later. Grief is like a journey, sometimes a long, difficult journey. But grief is a natural and healthy response to death.

Everyone grieves in their own way—some of us cry often; some of us cry very little. Grief takes time—months and years. Grief feelings can disappear and then return. Grief can make us feel tired or anxious. Grief can give us a headache or stomachache. After someone close to us dies, we may feel alone in our loss—even when we are surrounded by friends or people we love.

People die in many different ways. Some people die from an illness, such as cancer. Some people die suddenly from a heart attack or in a car accident. Some people die from violence in a shooting or war.

Some people die from a drug overdose or by suicide, which is when a person kills him- or herself. Most people who have died by suicide had a mental illness that confused the brain and made that person feel hopeless.

A grief journey is a difficult journey no matter how a person died. And after a person close to us dies, there are many changes. Adapting to change can be confusing and upsetting.

When someone dies and we are grieving, it can be helpful to talk to a teacher, a school counselor, or a social worker. It is also helpful to spend time with others who have experienced a death. A grief support group can help us cope and heal. In a grief support group, we can talk, listen, do activities together, and support one another.

Grief support groups, or bereavement groups, can be found in most communities. If someone important to you or close to you has died, speak to an adult you trust about finding a grief support group near you. No one should have to be alone in grief. Being together with others who have experienced a death can give us strength, hope, and tools for coping during the difficult grief journey.

1. Lehmann, Linda, Shane R. Jimerson, and Ann Gaasch. *Mourning Child Grief Support Group Curriculum*, 15.

Grief Support Resources

The Dougy Center (www.dougy.org) in Portland, Oregon, offers programs, professional training, activities, extensive online grief resources, and a search system for finding grief support groups throughout the United States and some other countries, including Japan.

The Children's Room (www.childrensroom.org) in Arlington, Massachusetts, offers on-site programs and online resources.

Hello Grief (www.hellogrief.org) offers information, including resources listed by state, and was started by Comfort Zone Camp (www.comfortzonecamp.org), which runs bereavement camps for children ages seven to seventeen, year-round, throughout the United States.

The National Alliance for Grieving Children (www.childrengrieve.org) is a network of support programs. NAGC has many online resources, including webinars and a child-caregiver activity book.

Selected Sources

Lehmann, Linda, Shane R. Jimerson, and Ann Gaasch. *Mourning Child Grief Support Group Curriculum: Early Childhood Edition*. Philadelphia: Brunner-Routledge, 2001.

Requarth, Margo. *After a Parent's Suicide: Helping Children Heal*. Sebastopol, CA: Healing Hearts Press, 2006.

Requarth, Margo. "Talking to Children about Suicide." *Grief Digest Magazine*, April 2007.

Schuurman, Donna. *Never the Same: Coming to Terms with the Death of a Parent*. New York: St. Martin's Press, 2003.

Sesame Workshop. *When Families Grieve*. New York: Sesame Street, 2010.

Silverman, Phyllis R., and Madelyn Kelly. *A Parent's Guide to Raising Grieving Children: Rebuilding Your Family after the Death of a Loved One*. New York: Oxford University Press, 2009.

Acknowledgments

With special thanks to Shelly Bathe Lenn, program director at The Garden: A Center for Grieving Children and Teens, in Northampton, Massachusetts; Deborah Rivlin and Christine Lambright of The Children's Room in Arlington, Massachusetts; and all those who shared their grief journeys with me. I wish everyone peace and resilience.

For Hannah and Josiah, with love always—HT

To my beautiful fiancé, Nicole, love you too x—AC

Library of Congress Cataloging-in-Publication data is on file with the publisher.

Text copyright © 2018 by Holly Thompson
Illustrations copyright © 2018 by Albert Whitman & Company
Illustrations by Ashley Crowley
First published in the United States of America in 2018 by Albert Whitman & Company
ISBN 978-0-8075-6112-6 (hardcover)
ISBN 978-0-8075-6113-3 (ebook)

Printed in China
10 9 8 7 6 WKT 28 27 26 25 24 23

For more information about Albert Whitman & Company,
visit our website at www.albertwhitman.com.